This book is **Dedicated** to our two children, **Wallace** and **James**. I would have loved to have read this book the *thousands of times* I'd rock and read you to sleep at night.

Photo By FIG Industries

About The Author

Dr. John R. Gerdy is founder and executive director of **Music For Everyone** (MusicForEveryone.org). He is also the author of several books on the role of sports, music and the arts in our schools and society. A lifelong musician, he has served as an "artist in residence" teaching the Blues to children from pre-K to grade 6. He performs regularly under the stage name **"Willie Marble."** To learn more about John, visit his website at **JohnGerdy.com**. To learn more about other products relating to the Alphabone Orchestra, please visit **AlphaboneOrchestra.com**.

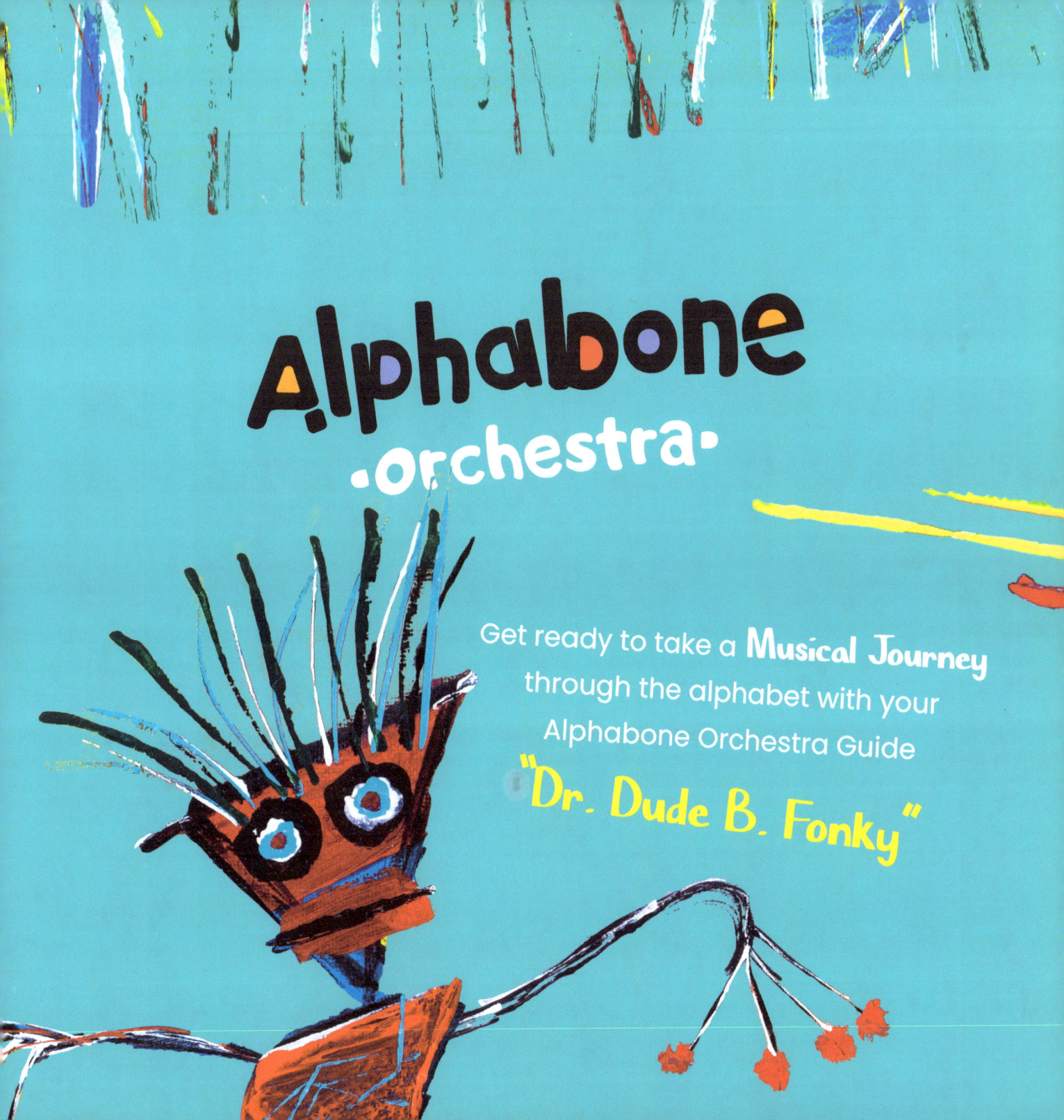

The **A-Bone** Alliance *Always* Accompanies **Accordions** on Acoustic Anthems *And* Arias.

GRACE NOTE:
An Accordion can sustain a note for longer than most instruments.

The **B-Bone** Belongs in **BIG BANDS** Booming, Bellowing and Blasting with a Bunch of Bagpipes, **Bassoons**, Bugles, Bells and Banjoes.

GRACE NOTE:
Long ago, bagpipes were used to scare people away during battle.

The **C-Bone** Club Can Include Clarinets, Cornets, Cellos, Crazy Cajons and *Crashing Cymbals*.

GRACE NOTE: Musical training develops language and math skills, improves memorization, instills discipline and nurtures creativity.

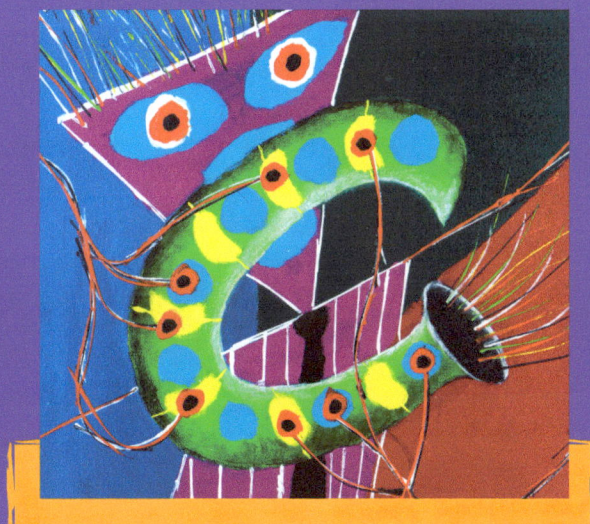

Dan the Dentist, Donna the Doctor and **Daffy Duck** all Dig the Dynamic, Deafening D-Bone.

GRACE NOTE:
Playing music is good for your heart.

GRACE NOTE: A song that gets stuck in your head is called an Earworm.

The **E-Bone** Ensemble *Enthusiastically* Entertained Everyone with an Excellent Example of an Enjoyable, **EXCITING ENCORE**.

The **F-Bone** Federation Flew to **France** For the Fantastic Flute Festival.

GRACE NOTE:
The Flute is the oldest instrument in the world to play notes.

The **G-Bone** Group Gathered their Gaggle of Green **GONGS**, Golden Glockenspiels and Grody Guitars with *Gusto*.

GRACE NOTE:
In German, Glockenspiel means 'to play the bells'.

GRACE NOTE:
The world's best selling instrument is the Harmonica.

The **H-Bone** is a **Heavy** Horn Humming in *Harmony* with Huge **HARPS** and Hushed Harmonicas.

The **I-Bone** Is

an Itty-Bitty but

Incredibly Interesting

and *Impressive*

Italian Instrument.

GRACE NOTE:
Playing in a music group or orchestra develops communication and Bandwork skills.

The Jumbo **J-Bone** Jubilee in June is in *Jamaica*.

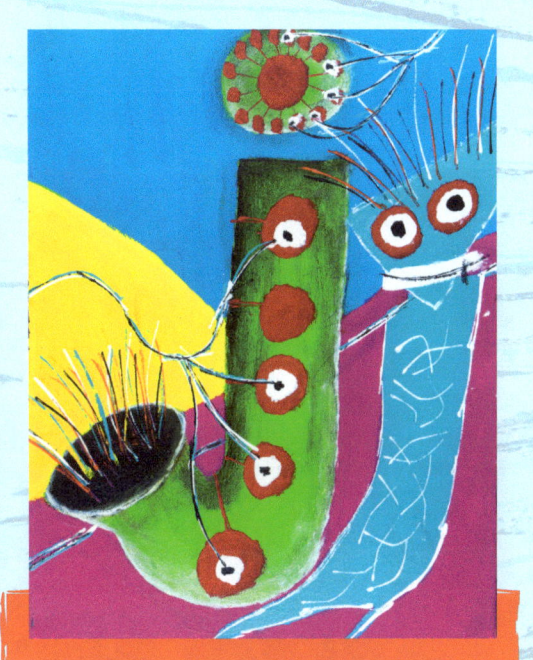

GRACE NOTE:
There are few activities in life that utilize the entire brain and music is one of them.

GRACE NOTE:
Multiple studies prove that singing in a group improves your mood.

The *Kooky Kangaroo* from Kalamazoo Kept his **K-Bone** and **Keyboard** on a Kayak in Kenya.

The **L-Bone** Looks Lovely in Lucy the Ladybug's Large *Louisiana* Laundromat.

GRACE NOTE: Music education leads to better test scores.

The **M-Bone** Mob *Marched* from Maine to Mexico with Many, Mini Muted **MANDOLINS**.

GRACE NOTE:
The Mandolin is considered one of the easier instruments to play.

Naturally, Nate from *Nantucket* and Ned from *Neptune* Never Needed their New **N-Bones** at Night.

GRACE NOTE:
"Jingle Bells," written by James Lord Pierpont in 1857, was originally meant to be sung during Thanksgiving.

GRACE NOTE:
A musician who plays the Oboe can be referred to as an Oboe Player or Oboist.

The Old **O-Bone** Orchestra played *Outrageous* Octaves with Odd Oboes and Offbeat Organs at the Ontario **OPERA**.

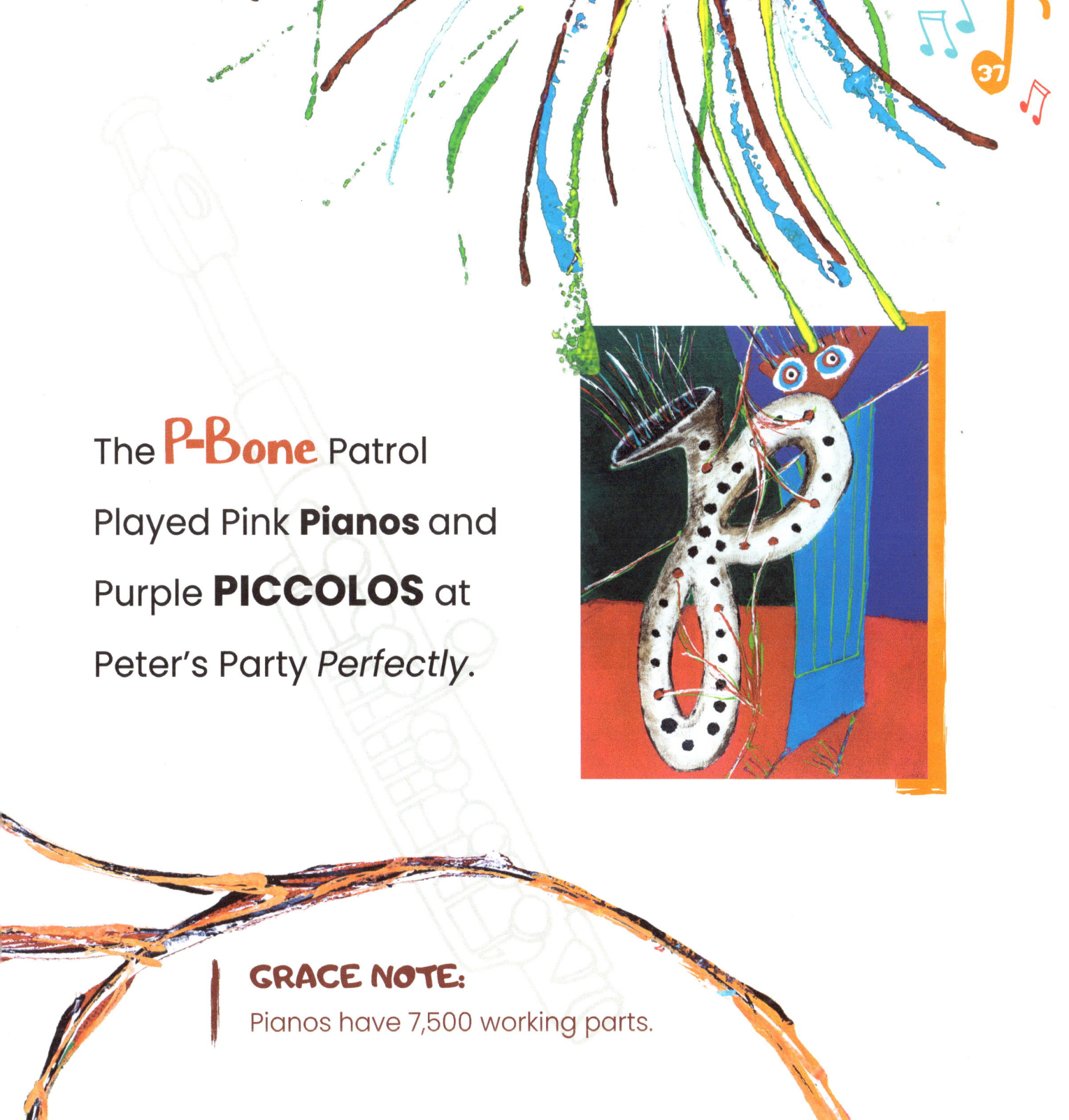

The **P-Bone** Patrol Played Pink **Pianos** and Purple **PICCOLOS** at Peter's Party *Perfectly*.

GRACE NOTE:
Pianos have 7,500 working parts.

The **Q-Bone Quartet** from Quebec was Quite *Quiet*.

GRACE NOTE:
Listening to music while exercising can significantly improve your workout performance.

Reggie the Red Rabbit *Regularly* Recorded **REGGAE** Records with His R-Bone on the Radio.

> **GRACE NOTE:**
> Playing music builds self-confidence.

GRACE NOTE:
Music helps plants grow faster.

The Society of **S-Bone** Sisters Sextet Sang Sonatas, Songs and Soprano Solos with the **SYMPHONY** of Silliness.

The **T-Bone** Team of Tiny Turtle Troubadours Tightly Tuned Their *Tamborines*, *Trumpets* and **TUBAS** Together.

GRACE NOTE: Most Tubas have about 16 feet of tubes.

The **UKULELE** Unit played in *Unison*

Under their Umbrellas in their Uniforms

at the **U-Bone** University.

GRACE NOTE:
The name Ukulele in Hawaiian means 'jumping flea'.

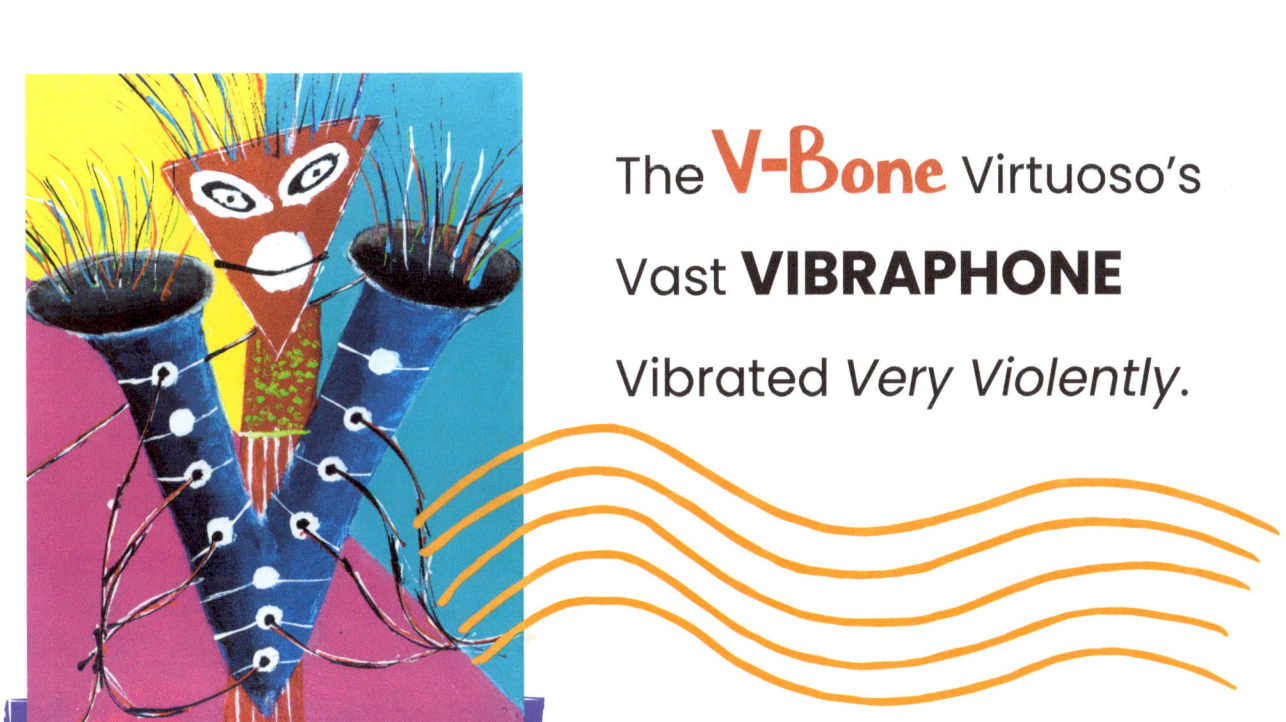

The **V-Bone** Virtuoso's Vast **VIBRAPHONE** Vibrated *Very Violently*.

GRACE NOTE:
The Vibraphone is considered a percussion instrument.

GRACE NOTE:
Not all Woodwinds are made of wood. Some are made of metal or plastic.

The **W-Bone** Waltz of Wee **WOODWINDS** Was *Weird, Wild and Wacky* When Whispered by Wally the Wildebeest.

X-Bones and XYLOPHONES

are eXcellent, eXciting, but *eXtremely* eXpensive.

GRACE NOTE:
Xylophones were used in Senegal to scare birds and monkeys out of fields and gardens.

The **Y-Bone** played by the Young Yellow Yak from Yonkers *Yowled* and *Yelped* in the Yard.

GRACE NOTE: Unborn babies hear and react to music.

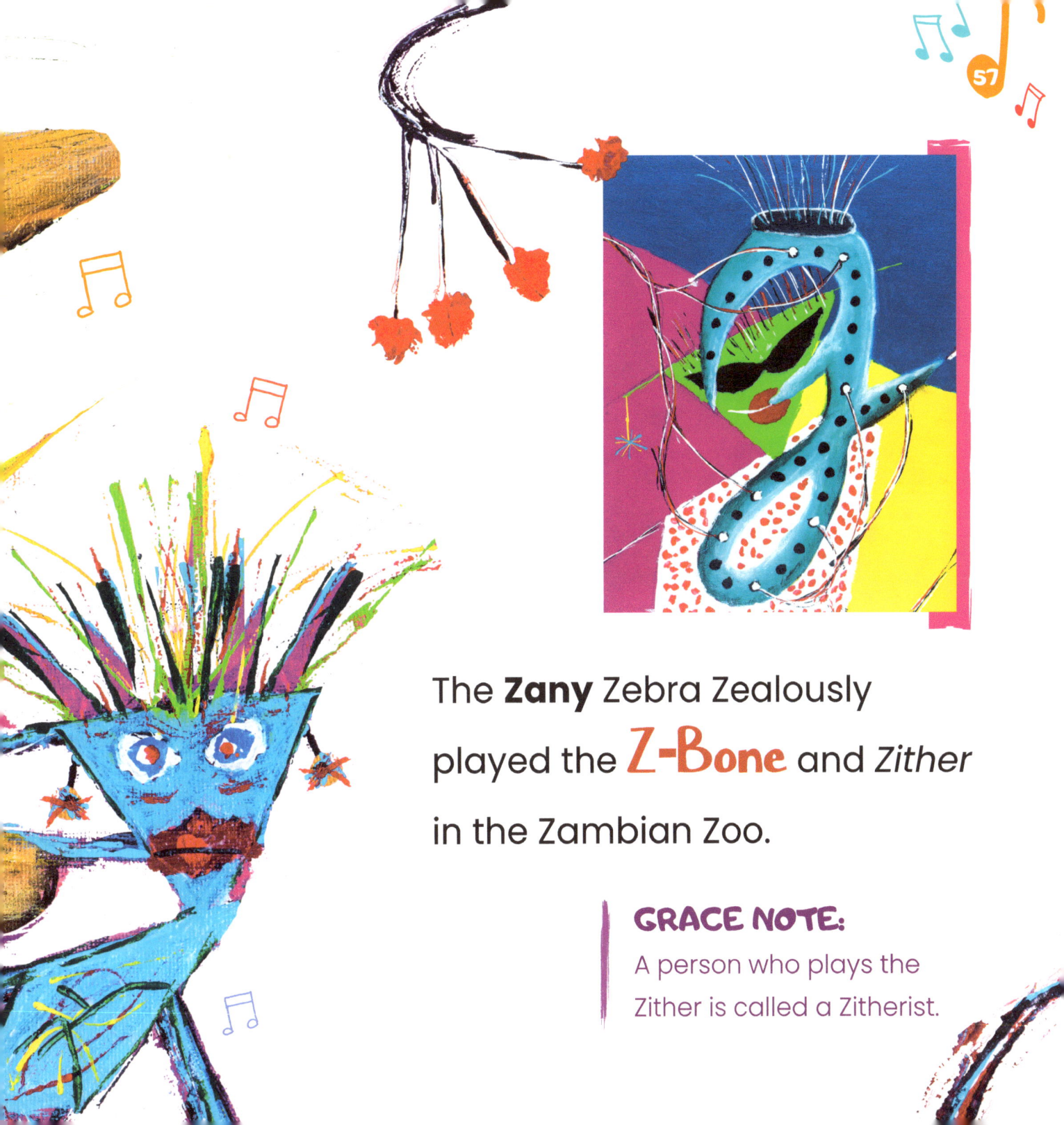

The **Zany** Zebra Zealously played the **Z-Bone** and *Zither* in the Zambian Zoo.

GRACE NOTE:
A person who plays the Zither is called a Zitherist.

Glossary of Musical Terms and Instruments

Accordion - a box-shaped instrument with bellows that make sounds when squeezed

Acoustic – a musical instrument not having electrical amplification

Anthem – a rousing or uplifting song identified with a particular group, body or cause

Aria – a song sung by a single voice, either with or without accompaniment

Bagpipes – Consist of an airbag connected to pipes that can be blown into and played like a flute

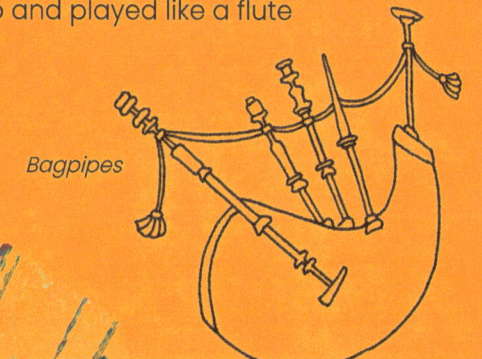

Bandwork – Similar to teamwork, bandwork is a cooperative effort by the members of a music group or band to achieve a common goal

Banjo - The banjo is a small four to six-stringed instrument with a long neck and a thin cover material stretched over a cylinder base

Bassoon - A large woodwind instrument that has a long hollow tube that creates low mellow sounds

Bell - a hollow cup that makes a ringing sound when struck

Blues – an African-American music that developed in the rural southern United States towards the end of the 19th century. Blues music can cover a wide range of emotions and musical styles, from slow sad songs of heartbreak and bad luck to raucous dance music that celebrates pleasure and success

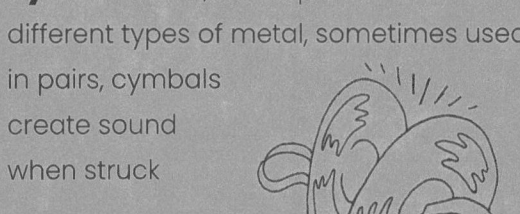

Bugle – a simple horn that has no valves, the pitch is controlled by the player's mouth

Cymbals – thin, round plates made of different types of metal, sometimes used in pairs, cymbals create sound when struck

Cajones – a box-shaped percussion instrument

Clarinet – a woodwind instrument that is tube-shaped, the player's hands can be used to cover holes along the sides of the tubes for pitch control

Encore – demand by an audience expressed by extended applause for an additional performance

Flute – a woodwind instrument that creates sound by the flow of air moving across its opening

Cello – a large 4 stringed instrument that is played with a bow, typically made from wood

Fonky – a strong musical rhythm or beat that has the soulful feeling of early Blues music; stylish and modern in an unconventional way

Cornet – a compact horn instrument that makes sounds by pushing air through tubes and valves

Dr. Dude B. Fonky – Famous musicologist who loves to study music wherever in the world it may take him; Also known as Dr. Fonky, he is a master of intrigue and disguise appearing in all shapes, sizes and colors

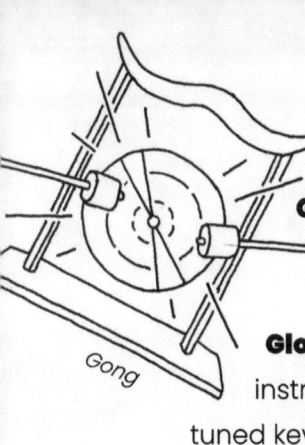

Gong – a flat, circular metal disc which is hit with a mallet

Glockenspiel – a percussion instrument made from a row of tuned keys

Grace Note – decorative note

Guitar – made up of a hollow chamber, strings, and fretting along a long neck

Harmony – the combination of musical notes played at the same time having a pleasing effect

Harp – a large stringed instrument that is played by the plucking of its stretched strings

Harmonica – a small rectangular box that is held to the lips and blown into the make sound

Keyboard – a row of keys that when struck, create sounds that go up in pitch from left to right

Mandolin – a stringed instrument that plays high pitch notes

Muted – to muzzle or soften the sound

Oboe – a woodwind instrument made of a large tube, sound is produced by the use of air pressure that the player creates

Octave – a tone that is eight full tones above or below another given tone

Opera – a theatrical presentation in which a dramatic performance is set to music

Orchestra – a large group of musicians who play together on various musical instruments, usually including strings, woodwinds, brass and percussion

Organ – a row of keys that when struck cause air to vibrate in a series of pipes that cause notes and volume to be produced

Piano – a row of keys that when struck, create sounds that go up in pitch from left to right

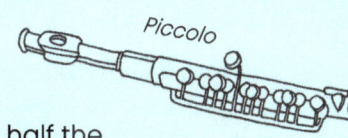

Piccolo – a flute but half the size, creates a higher-pitched sound

Quartet – a group of four performing musicians

Reggae – a style of popular music originating in Jamaica which became widely known in the 1970s through the work of Bob Marley

Sextet – a group of six performing musicians

Sonata – a song for an instrumental soloist, often with piano accompaniment, typically in several parts

Soprano – the highest natural human voice found in some women and young boys

Symphony – an elaborate musical composition for a full orchestra

Tambourine – a round frame with small flat metal discs built into it, which create a 'jingle' sound when the frame is struck

Troubadours – the poet-musicians of France about the twelfth century who often sang love songs

Trumpet – a brass instrument with valves

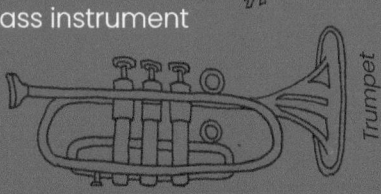

Tuba – a low pitch instrument with a large hollow tube that opens up like a cone at the end

Ukulele – a small guitar-like instrument with a higher pitch sound

Unison – When two or more voices or instruments sound exactly the same note.

Vibraphone – made of tuned metal bars, and is played by holding two or four soft mallets and striking the bars to create sound

Virtuoso – a person highly skilled in music or another artistic pursuit

Waltz – a dance performed in triple time by a couple, who as a pair turn rhythmically around and around as they progress around the dance floor

Woodwinds – the orchestral wind-instruments that include bassoons, clarinets, flutes, oboes and sometimes saxophones

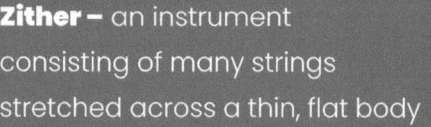

Xylophone – a percussion instrument that consists of wooden bars that are struck by mallets to create sound

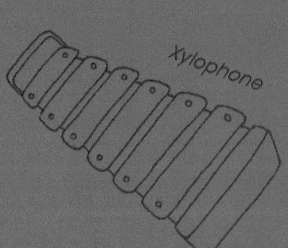

Zither – an instrument consisting of many strings stretched across a thin, flat body

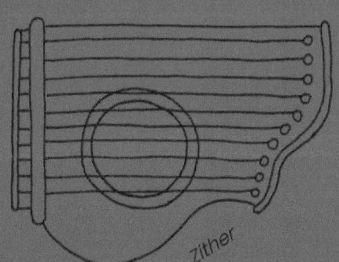

Alphabone
orchestra

An enormous **"Thank You"** to my art teacher, Loryn Spangler-Jones (LSJStudios.com) for inspiring me to stretch myself in undertaking a new art form and challenging me to have the courage to never be afraid to *"color outside the lines."* And to all of the folks at Kinectiv (getkinectiv.com). Your creativity took this project to a level that I could have never imagined. It has been a pleasure to work with all of you.

A percentage of the proceeds from
the sale of this book will be donated to:

Music For Everyone
(MusicForEveryone.org)

and the

Lancaster Early Education Center
(LancasterEarlyEducation.org)

Copyright © 2019 by Gerdsong Productions
All rights reserved. This book or any portion thereof
may not be reproduced or used in any manner whatsoever
without the express written permission of the author/publisher
except for the use of brief quotations in a book review.
Printed in the United States of America
First Printing, 2019
ISBN 978-0-578-59684-6
Gerdsong Productions
Lancaster, PA
www.AlphaboneOrchestra.com

CPSIA information can be obtained
at www.ICGtesting.com
Printed in the USA
BVHW021215151022
649335BV00002B/25